DON'T
TOUCH THE
NUTS

GENTS

DON'T
TOUCH THE
NUTS

**AND OTHER UNWRITTEN RULES
OF THE BRITISH PUB**

DANIEL FORD

Published in 2010 by New Holland Publishers (UK) Ltd
London • Cape Town • Sydney • Auckland
www.newhollandpublishers.com

Garfield House, 86–88 Edgware Road, London W2 2EA, United Kingdom
80 McKenzie Street, Cape Town 8001, South Africa
Unit 1, 66 Gibbes Street, Chatswood, NSW 2067, Australia
218 Lake Road, Northcote, Auckland, New Zealand

10 9 8 7 6 5 4 3 2 1

A catalogue record for this book is available from the British Library

ISBN 978 1 84773 704 5

Senior Editor: Kate Parker
Editorial Direction: Rosemary Wilkinson
Publisher: Aruna Vasudevan
Editorial Assistance: Eloise Wood
Design and cover design: Vanessa Green, The Urban Ant Ltd
Illustrations: Tom Hughes
Production: Melanie Dowland

Reproduction by Pica Digital Pte. Ltd., Singapore
Printed and bound in India by Replika Press

To all my locals over the years . . .

*The Prince Albert (Greenwich), The Hufflers Arms (Dartford),
The Wheatsheaf (Headley), The White Horse (Oxford),
Charlie's Bar (Paphos, Cyprus) and
The Royal Oak (Cape Town, South Africa).*

CONTENTS

INTRODUCTION

This introduction is being written in a pub. My publishers would expect nothing less, I have decided. Plus, I fancied a pint. More importantly, I fancied looking around at other people and wondering what the hell they are doing here rather than being in work at 11.14am on a Tuesday (like me). I'm also pondering whether I can claim this beer on expenses.

'Can I get a receipt for that, please?'

'A receipt for a pint of Foster's?!' replies the barmaid.

'That's right.'

'What kind of job lets you claim beer on expenses?'

'Ah, well, I'm writing a book on pubs, you know.'

'Right love, and Dave over there is a rocket scientist.'

I may be wrong, but I suspect she's taking the piss. Although I also suspect pubs were probably invented so we had somewhere to take the piss out of each other.

'Taking the piss' is a British obsession, right up there with updates on the weather and endless cups of tea. And where better to start a book on the unwritten rules of pubs than with rule number one?

You can, as a rule, take the piss out of people in a pub to an extent you could never get away with on the street. However, as with all rules, there are exceptions:

- If the other person is bigger than you
- If you are wearing a cravat

It's 11.58am and two builders have just walked in. At least they've been to work first, unlike Dave and the other people sitting at the bar.

'Can I claim this second beer on expenses do you reckon?' I ask them. 'I'm writing a book on pubs, you see.'

'Sure,' says the big one.

'And Dave over there is a rocket scientist,' says the one wearing a cravat.

'Hang on, hang on,' I wail. 'I've used all that material. How am I going to complete this book if I'm using the same stuff already?'

They ignore me.

I decide I should hang around a bit longer, just so this introduction is authentic, you understand.

The builders have downed their beers and left already. Good old swift ones. Swift ones are not so much a rule as a custom. Me? I'm not much of a 'swift one' type of guy; for me, pubs are to be enjoyed, savoured. Nevertheless, I can accept people, like the builders, who are on a short break and fancy a quick pint, a packet of crisps and a check on the cricket score; but what's with those people who come in, order a double vodka and down it before their change is out of the till? I mean, that's just mainlining alcohol. What's the point? You might as well just keep a bottle in your drawer at work.

It's 1.26pm and a few people have come in for lunch. The special is pork chops.

'Would you like a receipt for that too, love,' asks the barmaid (her name's Clare she tells me; I think I might have pulled). 'For your expenses?'

She's now warming to the idea of this book, especially as I just bought her half a lager, and I now know Dave is actually a life insurance salesman and Tuesday is his day off. He apparently comes in every week, has breakfast, reads his *Telegraph*, disappears to put his bets on and comes back to do some work (that's what Clare reckons anyway, because he's always on the phone and writing notes). Later, he just talks rubbish, plays darts with his friends and gets drunk.

In Dave's day off I have found the perfect summary of why the British love pubs. Ah, thank goodness I stayed here. Everyone knows pubs are central to life in Britain and Dave's day off shows why. In just one day his local is his restaurant, his library, his office and his social meeting place. If he'd just put some money in the jukebox and pull the barmaid (not Clare, she's too nice for Dave) then he'd never need to leave the pub at all.

The reason most of us like pubs is that it's a home from home (without the nagging partner or screaming children). The heating is on (and it's not your bill), the telly is on (and it's not your subscription), there are snacks available whenever you want them, and the fridge never runs out of cold beer (except on New Year's Eve). But best of all, in this wonderful nation where social interaction is awkward to say the least, this is a place where you can enjoy the company of other people, or simply feel a part of a group. Is it any wonder that the writers of most British soaps use the pub as the pivot of their plots? You simply don't get it in US or Aussie soaps. In those, people actually visit each other's homes. Heaven forbid!

We Brits do pubs better than anyone, let's be honest. In fact, apart from the Irish and the odd enclave dotted around the English-speaking world, we are pretty much the only ones who do pubs at

all. Elsewhere it's all pavement cafes, bistros and bars. But to really enjoy a pub you have to know how it works. You have to know what pubs you can and can't go in, where you can and can't sit, what to drink, who you can and can't talk to and, most importantly of all, which urinal you can piss in.

I've got a Colombian friend, Carlos, who reckons British pubs are like foreign islands in what (to him) is already a foreign island – a bit like Guernsey to the rest of us, maybe?

'In Colombia,' he says, 'we too meet friends and have a drink. But I can't work your pubs out. It's all a bit confusing to understand what's going on.'
Be confused no more. Pubs are run by a set of complex rules, but over time they can be understood. These are not rules you will find hung on the wall, however; they are unwritten. Well, at least they were until I started this book.

Sorry, must go, Clare's smiling at me. Think I'll stay for one more.

Daniel Ford, Greenwich, South London, 3.27pm, one summer(ish) Tuesday afternoon

THE WHITE HART OR THE COUNTRY SQUIRE?

Which pub is for you?

There are, basically, eight types of pubs, but within these categories there is a lot of overlap – you may well find a student pub near a harbour, for instance – and lots of sub-sections – music pubs, theme pubs and so on – but, for simplicity's sake, let's stick to the main eight.

1. The Local

All pubs are, to a certain extent, local pubs. However, a true local (often referred to as a 'real local') can be identified by one hard-and-fast rule: the moment you push open the door everyone stops talking and turns to look at you. Even the jukebox pauses. This is not the time to break step or ask if they serve risotto; simply march to the bar, nod at the nearest person, mutter 'alwite' and order the strongest lager on tap. 'Locals' tend to be in areas where people can walk to the pub, thus attracting the same bunch every night. As a rule, a local is sparsely decorated, has a darts team, shows the football on the TV at all times, and is never known by its full name

– for example, The White Hart would be just 'the Hart' and the Stag's Head would be known as 'the Stag's'. Interestingly, often you only have to go into the same pub three or four times and you too will be a local and allowed to stare at unsuspecting newcomers who stumble through the door.

2. Inner-city pubs

Surprise, surprise, these are found in the inner cities. Bereft of any architectural appeal or decor, they must have boarded-up windows and blood on the walls. They are usually named after the local area with the simple addition of 'Arms' – as in 'Why-The-Hell-Does-Anyone-Live-Here Arms'.

3. Harbour pubs

See 'Inner-city pubs' above except these pubs are located by a harbour. They all have to be called The Ship or The Anchor;

if the pub is particularly interesting it is allowed to be called The Ship and Anchor.

Harbour pubs are never called the Seaman's anything, for obvious reasons.

4. Country pubs

At best, this will be a beautiful 16th-century inn where you can impress a date; at worst it will be a

carvery overrun with children on Sundays. The former must have old benches where you can sit and stare over the fields/river/hills while chatting about how lovely it would be to live in the country; while it is obligatory for the latter to have a mini-Disneyland in the garden.

Country pubs have a lot of wood in them, and must claim to have had a famous person stay there once (take your pick from Charles Dickens, King George I/II/III/IV, William Shakespeare or Sven-Goran Eriksson).

If nobody famous actually stayed at the pub then the back-up rule is that it must have a ghost.

Names need to be countrified, such as The Country Squire, The Fox and Hounds or The Pheasant Inn. None are called The Pheasant Plucker, as far as I know.

5. Gastropubs

These are places that make more money from food than drink and therefore should not even be called pubs.

6. Tourist pubs

Have you ever been to an Irish theme pub in another country? Well, that pretty much sums up tourist pubs, although they're often not quite as kitsch. Tourist pubs are found in places such as Oxford, Cambridge, York and the touristy parts of London. The main qualifying factor for a tourist pub is that, although most of the customers are foreign, none of the bar staff (even if they are foreign themselves) are allowed to understand a foreign accent or speak anything but English. Be prepared to wait 20 minutes to get served as the other customers grapple with their English, ask about the various merits of each (allegedly warm) beer, then finally order 16 plates of 'traditional' fish and chips before disappearing outside to find out what table number their party is sitting on.

7. Student pubs

Yes, you've got it, a pub where students go. Characterised by cheap prices, these pubs must have beer-stained tables and chairs and lots of things to keep young minds active, such as pool and darts and table-football; a quiz machine is an absolute essential, although you're more likely to find a hotbed of drunkenness than intellectual debate here.

8. JD Wetherspoons

These pubs deserve their own category for their noble mission of renovating some great old buildings and providing food and drink at great prices (which often act to drive prices down in nearby pubs as well). Please note, however, that they must not have music or any atmosphere whatsoever.

'Harbour pubs are never called the Seaman's anything, for obvious reasons.'

The 10 Most Common Pub Names

1. The Crown
2. The Red Lion
3. The Royal Oak
4. The Swan
5. The White Hart
6. The Railway
7. The Plough
8. The White Horse
9. The Bell
10. The Forcit Inn

* Source: CAMRA (OK, I made the last one up)

'HE'S NEXT...'

The rituals of queuing and buying a round

The queue

Everyone knows the British like queuing but only we could form a queue when there is no queue. It is sometimes known as 'the queue that no one can see but everyone knows exists' (snappy, eh?), i.e. everyone knows whose turn it is next even though there is no physical queue. It works like this:

☞ You approach the bar, hold out your money, open your eyes wide in expectation and generally use all your body-language skills to show that you are waiting to be served. The alternative method of shouting, 'Oi! Get your fat arse over here, I'm dying of thirst,' I've never found to be very successful.

☞ While doing this, you must scan the full-length of the bar to see who is already waiting. You don't need to know who is next, but you must know who is before you. (If two of you approach the bar at exactly the same time, you must arm-wrestle to decide who is next. OK, I made this up, but if enough of us start doing it then it could catch on.)

☞ If a bartender approaches you for your order out of turn you must point and mutter, 'he's next' or, if you are feeling chatty, 'this man was before me', even if that person is right at the other end of the bar. This will elicit a grunt of appreciation and you'll get a nice warm feeling inside (although that might be the whisky).

☞ If someone else is actually 'before' the guy you have elected then that is his job to say so, not yours. You have done your queue duty, and when your turn comes you can rest easy in the knowledge that everyone else will grunt in your direction and you will get served. Don't feel guilty, just feel happy that the rest of them are now enjoying that same warm feeling you had a few moments ago. Spread the love.

'"He's Next" will elicit a grunt of appreciation and you'll get a nice warm feeling inside (although that might be the whisky).'

There are some specific exceptions to this rule:

☞ Just because someone is sitting at the bar does not mean he is in the queue. You must assess how much beer he has left in his glass; a rule of thumb is that any more than a third of a pint means he is simply drinking at the bar, any less than that and he has magically joined the queue. Those under 40 might straighten their back and raise their heads up like a Meerkat to show they are back in the queue; older drinkers simply raise their glass or tip it towards the pump as if they are Oliver Twist asking for more.

The regulars, especially the Old Boys, will usually get served in-between the rest of the queue. They don't need to ask, or even raise their eyebrows, but their Guinness will be pulled just as you take your eye off the ball and turn to ask your girlfriend which flavour crisps she fancies.

☞ As pubs get busier the queues are split into sections as the barman can't be expected to keep an eye on the whole bar, but simply a section of it. The busier it gets the smaller your section. So, in a really busy pub, although it would be rude to go ahead of the bloke next to you, ignoring someone a couple of metres away is fine. In a particularly rammed pub, it's every drinker for himself. Note that this is still not the signal to shout, 'Oi! Get your fat arse over here, I'm dying of thirst.'

☞ Towards the end of the evening, as everyone gets drunk, the queue becomes more fluid and at last orders it disappears completely.

☞ If you jump the queue by accident but only realise it as your lager shandy (which must be what you're drinking if you made such an obvious mistake) is being poured, you must apologise and make a half-hearted attempt to 'get back in line'. The barman will ignore your pleas but at least you have shown willing and you can now chat to the injured party about how long you have both been standing there, and use phrases such as 'ridiculous wait', 'slow today', 'need more staff' and so on. As you take your change you must tell the barman that your new friend is 'next'. You now have a common bond of misunderstanding and are allowed to strike up a proper conversation later in the evening.

If you queue jump without the appropriate apology you will get stared at and maybe even grunted at – this is the worst possible thing that can happen to someone from Britain.

Buying rounds

Oh, the etiquette of rounds. The rules for this are almost as complex as the urinal rules (*see* page 99) and just as dangerous if you get them wrong. As with most pub rules (in fact, as with most British social rules), everyone pretends they are relaxed about the whole process but don't you believe it. People are counting, watching and taking stock of everything you are doing and saying. So … read 'em and have your wallet to the ready:

☛ If someone offers you a drink and you are genuinely just staying for one, you can say that and buy your own. If pushed, however, then it is traditional to accept the drink while saying, 'I'll get you one next time', allowing the buyer to generously proclaim, 'Don't be daft, forget about it.' Don't forget. Next time you see him it will be silently known by both of you that it is your round. Needless to say, if you don't just stay for one drink (does anyone?) then it's your round next.

'As with most pub rules, everyone pretends they are relaxed about the whole process, but don't you believe it.'

☛ Another reason to not join a round is if you are skint. In this situation most people will use a euphemism such as, 'No it's alright, I'm drinking on my own', and trust that their sad face and the holes in their jeans convey the message. It is okay to accept a sympathy drink, but only one.

☞ If you win any money in the pub (Lottery bonus ball, football scratch card, raffle, etc.) you will be expected to buy a round even if the round costs more than your winnings – serves you right for being lucky. Be warned: if you win money in the bookies and you announce it in the pub you will also be expected to share your good fortune with a round. When you lose (as is usual) your friends will not buy you a round in sympathy. Funny that.

☞ If someone announces he is buying everyone a drink because his football team just won the cup, his wife has had a baby (don't ask if he's sure it's his) then that doesn't count as his round. This is extra and the round will resume where it paused before the grand gesture.

☞ Someone always has to buy the first round; make sure you take your turn sometimes. It's bad form to wait for the last round in the hope that some people drop off and you save money. Some people fear they will lose out by buying the first round, however scientific research has shown this is not true (although I can't for the life of me remember where I read that). If someone always waits for the last round then just as he orders quickly drag a couple of new people into the round and (on his behalf) declare very loudly that all the bar staff

'If you win any money in the pub, you will be expected to buy a round even if the round costs more than your winnings – serves you right for being lucky.'

can have a drink and that the change should go in the charity box for local orphans. He will be too embarrassed to back down.

☞ Don't take the piss by ordering double whiskies when everyone else is on lager.

☞ If it's your round and everyone is feeling peckish you will be expected to get the crisps in. Always remember the rule on page 65 and ask the barman to list the entire selection of crisps before plumping for six packets of cheese and onion – your group is expected to laugh when the barman gets annoyed.

☞ Couples do not count as one person when it comes to rounds.

☞ If you buy a member of the bar staff a drink when they are working they are not expected to buy one back (because the drink is the equivalent of a tip), but if they are sitting on your side of the bar they should join the round like anyone else.

☞ Everyone will deny keeping a check on who pays their way, yet the phrase 'short arms, long pockets' for someone who ducks out of buying their share is a well known one.

☞ There is some genuine leeway among close friends when it comes to rounds as things balance out in the long term.

Other than those few rules when it comes to rounds, you've nothing to worry about. No one's that bothered, really. Except, come to think of it, my mate Pete does still owe me a pint from that time in the Dragon in 1997. Pete, next time you're in …

'TWO PINTS OF BITTER AND A LAGER TOP'

What does your drink say about you?

Know what you want to drink

Those new to drinking (where have you been?) or to this country (Bonjour! Hola! Ciao!) reveal their lack of knowledge when it comes to pubs by asking simply for 'a beer'. 'This is a bloody pub, beer is what pubs sell!', I feel like screaming at them. Those optics and all those bottles filled with coloured liquids are just for show. 'Beer, beer, beer!' It's the equivalent of going into a restaurant and asking for 'a plate of food', or to a cinema and asking for 'two tickets to a film' (adding 'please', of course, this being Britain).

At the very least you must know what type of beer you want – lager, bitter, light ale and so on – but really you should know exactly the beer you want and order it by name. All self-respecting drinkers will stick with the same drink, which enables them to simply ask for 'the same again' or allows the bartender to say 'the usual'. Note, there is no question mark after 'the usual' because it is not actually a question, even though it may appear to be one. It is simply part of the social routine between bartender and customer. She may as well say, 'Hello Dan, I am about to pour what you always drink, you boring sod.' Ordering the same drink every night also has the added bonus of keeping things simple: you never have to think when you're drunk and it helps the bartender if he's a bit thick.

Tourists also compound their mistake by asking for a 'large' or 'small' beer. It is only ever a pint or a half (or a bottle). The old rule of pints for men and halves for women is fast fading out, which really is bad news as it pushes up the cost of a round by 25 per cent (you're working it out now, aren't you?). Having a half is a bit of a minefield. Although it's acceptable to have a swift half before heading home after having downed six pints you should generally not order a half unless:

☛ You only have £1.45 in your pocket.

☛ You appear interested in the guest ales and want to taste them all. You can only get away with this if you have a beard and are wearing walking boots.

☛ You are a regular and the bar staff don't actually measure out the half, instead choosing to simply top up your pint glass by estimating a half. All wily customers know to take an extra gulp just before the bartender takes your glass thus ensuring you get a bit extra. The trick is not to be greedy.

So, it's pretty straightforward really. Know what you want to drink and order it by name, and only order it in quantities of pints (or, in the circumstances named above, halves).

There is just one more thing to be considered: if you want to set yourself apart from the crowd you can add something extra to your beer. Acceptable extras are lemonade (a top), blackcurrant (a bit studenty) and lime (old school). Unacceptable extras are cherries, chunks of pineapple and umbrellas – keep it to Majorca if you really must.

'Acceptable extras are lemonade, blackcurrant and lime. Unacceptable extras are cherries, chunks of pineapple and umbrellas – keep it to Majorca if you really must.'

Choosing your drink

Choose your drink carefully because you will soon be branded and it is hard to change it down the line. In my local I was previously known as Foster's Dan, who drank with Guinness Tom. In a pub, you are what you drink, so be careful what you chose …

Normal lager

This is commonly known as 'session' beer – in other words you can drink it all day long, if that is your thing. Containing around four per cent alcohol by volume (abv), this covers Carlsberg, Carling, Foster's and Stella 4s. In pubs that don't carry these mainstream beers (such as Samuel Smith pubs), it is acceptable to say 'A pint of Foster's equivalent, please', and the barman will match you up with a beer you have never heard of, which usually has a picture of Heidi's grandad surrounded by mountains on the tap.

Strong lager

Now, why would you drink strong lager? Yes, that is correct: to get pissed. It's only one per cent stronger than the above but for some reason that one per cent blows your head off. Not for nothing do the mind-altering effects of strong lager cause each to have its own nickname, the most famous of which being 'wife beater'. Please note: if you drink more than three strong lagers you will immediately be tagged a 'binge drinker'.

Bitter

You need to be over 50 and constantly sneering at the lager drinkers, reminding them that lager is not real beer, English, or made properly – whatever that means.

Real ale

To drink these you, too, need to be over 50, wear corduroy trousers and have bits of spittle in your beard. As a real-ale drinker you never know what you want, preferring to study the array of ales on offer as you enter the pub. You are allowed to discuss the various merits of each ale with the bartender ('Old Sock's Ale from Bridlington, now that's the fruity one, is it?') but, best of all, you are allowed to ask for a taster before ordering. Note: It is not acceptable to taste all the real ales on offer then ask for a Carling top.

Shandy

Can be ordered after football training only.

Mild

You must be 83 or over.

Light and bitter or Light and lager

Heaven knows why anyone still adds light ale to their lager or bitter. Those who do so usually say it's because that's what they first drank with their uncle and they haven't changed yet. Time to move on boys.

A bottle of beer

If you order a bottle of beer you must drink out of it and always be standing. When turning down the offer of a glass you can exclaim 'But it's already in a glass!' Ho ho. Bottles of beer are also good for those who fancy stumbling around to the jukebox later in the evening when the alcohol kicks in but don't have the confidence to let go of their drink.

Cider

The Cider House Rules (ho ho) have changed dramatically in the last few years thanks to Bulmers. How one brand of cider changed the rules is beyond everyone, but it is now cool to load up a glass with ice and top up with cider. Previous rules for drinking cider still stand (i.e. you must be a student, speak with a West Country accent when you take your first sip or be sitting in a pub garden), but the glass-full-of-ice rule is now the king even in winter.

'It is not acceptable to taste all the real ales on offer then ask for a Carling top.'

Guinness

You must be Irish, a wannabe Irish, or claim Irish ancestory. That'll be half the world then. Whichever one you are you must exclaim, 'Of course, it's not as good as the real stuff in Dublin!', even if you have never been there. The brewers of Guinness have built up a whole set of rules regarding the pouring of a pint, with precise timings for each stage; therefore, Guinness drinkers are the only ones allowed, of all the drinkers, to advise bar staff where they are going wrong in the pouring process.

Alcopops

It is acceptable for men under the age of 21 or women of any age to drink an alcopop at anytime (although I've never seen an

alcopop being drunk in the morning). Anyone else ordering one must explain his reason. 'I fancied one for a change' is a good enough explanation to have the first one. 'I've had enough beer', while rubbing your tongue round your mouth to show you need to sweeten up the bitter taste, is good enough for ordering a second one. There is never an acceptable reason to drink three.

Non-alcoholic beer

You can order this if you are driving or taking antibiotics. You are allowed to comment that although it's not like the real thing, you can't face drinking Coke all night.

Soft drinks

Even the name (soft) we give to these drinks gives a clue of what we think of them. Women or drivers are allowed soft drinks. If you are the latter it will be necessary every time you order a drink (and every time you pick up the soft drink to take a sip) to look around the pub and reassure everyone 'I'm driving tonight.' You are also allowed to use the antibiotics excuse, but only once a year. This is because no one really believes you anyway and if you actually do have a raging yeast infection, we'd rather not drink with you until it's cleared up.

Water

This can be ordered after a heavy night for rehydration but it must be accompanied by a pint. In certain pubs (poncey ones) it is also okay to have a glass of water before heading home.

Tea or coffee

Hmmm. What exactly are you doing in a pub?

'CAN I HAVE A STRAIGHT GLASS?'

Which glass to use for which drink

Different beer glasses

So, you've ordered a beer, now what could be simpler than drinking it? Hey, hold your horses, haven't you considered what glass you want it in? Poor, poor old tourists, not only do they have to order in a foreign language (yes, you may be surprised, but in many parts of the world English is actually a foreign language), choose the exact beer they want, know to order it in pints, but then ∴ oh the joy … they may also be given a choice of glass to have it in.

Most beers have their own special glasses, produced by the maker of the beer, so that should be simple enough. In fact, apparently there's even a law that a beer has to be served in its own branded glass unless the drinker asks otherwise (lawyers would call it 'passing off' if it's not done, although can you seriously imagine anyone being prosecuted for putting a Carling in a Foster's glass?) Do drinkers really care? Boy oh boy, do they. So what are your choices, assuming you don't take the default trade glass?

A personalised tankard

This is a throwback to the 1950s and earlier, when regulars kept their own drinking utensil (often with their name engraved on it) behind the bar at their local to set them apart form the casual drinker who used the pub glasses. Think of it as playing golf with your own clubs as opposed to borrowing a set each time you play a round. Put that way, it's a wonder the habit died out, really. Nevertheless, tankards, usually made of pewter, are now probably the naffest thing you can drink from, unless you're in fancy dress at a Viking theme night on a long table. At this point I should confess I have a tankard down my local. Now, before you stop reading and burn this book in shame, I should explain. I received the tankard (engraved with my name, yes, yes) from my football club as an end-of-season recognition for my efforts. Now what do I do? Put it on the mantelpiece (I don't even have a mantelpiece) or use the thing? And therein lies the reason why I have a tankard behind the bar and why my nickname in the pub has changed from Foster's Dan (*see* page 30) to Tankard Dan. Stop sniggering, it's not big and it's not clever. So, in conclusion, you need to be either aged 79 or called Dan to use a tankard.

Straight glass

Absolutely nothing to do with your sexual orientation – although it always gets a 'boom, boom' in my local gay pub. You should choose this if you are one of the lager-drinking masses at the younger end of the market (i.e. under 30). It is not strictly straight (stop sniggering), but in fact slightly angled so the glass holds more beer at the top than the bottom. You have a choice between the classic straight glass and the relatively new invention that has little raised dots on the inside of the base and is said to 'keep the bubbles flowing throughout the drinking experience'. Well, that's what the PR people would say anyway.

Bell-end glass

Not the official name but it makes me laugh. This was formally known as the straight glass and is the glass that has a bubble three-quarters of the way up, only, as far as I can imagine to help the drinker grip the glass when he's had one too many. Use this if you are an older lager drinker and grew up with these glasses or if you like bitter but prefer to look younger than the jug (*see* opposite page) users.

The giant bell-end

Snigger, snigger. This oversized glass, really a tulip glass (think extra big Guinness glass), has emerged from the growth in the ice-and-cider market and is to accommodate all that ice while still giving some space for the liquid. Use this glass if you order a cider with ice in it. Er, that's it.

Jugs

Cue another *Carry On*-style laugh. This is the glass with a handle and panels on the side, the sort of glass that makes me think of monks for some reason. Those big jolly monks, with fat, round bellies, rosy cheeks and a liking for ale. You need to drink bitter or, preferably, real ale to use these glasses and be at least 50. The other rule is that drinkers who use the half-pint jug must accept they look ridiculous; no particular reason, they just do.

The bottle

Just because a drink comes in a bottle doesn't mean you can always drink it from the bottle. It is acceptable to drink from the bottles of the self-styled classy beers (Budvar, Peroni, etc.) but it must be held label-outwards and at chest height to ensure your wealth of culture is displayed to the masses drinking the draught lagers. It is not okay to drink from the bottle if you order a Newcastle Brown Ale or light ale (that's just wrong), beers that are trying-but-just-can't-quite-make-the-designer-level (Budweiser) or any Belgian beer (as they all have their own special glasses anyway).

Drinking from the bottle is also the only time you are allowed a piece of fruit in your drink. This is because certain beers, such as the Mexican Corona or Sol, traditionally come with a wedge of lemon or lime in the neck of the bottle. At this point you are allowed to confirm your worldliness to everyone by saying, 'They do this in Mexico to keep the flies out of the beer, you know.' Just ignore the fact that it is minus two degrees outside and that no one has seen a fly for three months.

New for old?

Finally, assuming you don't just stop for one beer, you must decide if you are a 'Fresh glass, please' drinker or 'Same glass, please' drinker. This depends on your view of cleanliness: is it better to trust the pub dishwasher or just regurgitate your own germs?

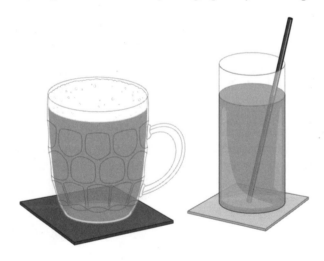

Discussions can be had each time you order a pint. Either way, once you've made your choice stick with it or people will think you are indecisive and, believe me, in a pub that is a lot worse than actually getting the lurgy.

Sending a pint back

I am tempted to say don't send pints back, but generally (and I have just returned from a survey of pubs – all in the name of research you'll understand) landlords say that if you are polite and don't make a fuss you'll get a new beer poured if you think there is something wrong with the first one. However, you can't send a pint back:

- ☞ For a refund

- ☞ If you have drunk more than half of it

- ☞ If you have been staring at it for more than five minutes and holding it up to the light for inspection. Mick, the landlord in my local, calls that 'drinking with your eyes'.

Sending a half pint back is a risky strategy, as you've already aroused suspicion by ordering a half. You don't want to look like you *don't like beer*. Just suck it up and order something different next time.

'THAT'S CHARLIE'S SEAT'

Old Boys and other locals

The Old Boy

There's a pub on the Isle of Dogs in East London that I go to sometimes. I've never seen more than five people in the place at once, although it's pretty big so maybe it gets busy late at night. I prefer to sit at the short end of the bar near the door like Billy No Mates. I'm usually reading my paper, so I bother no one and no one bothers me. Until twenty to seven that is. That's when the barmaid or arbitrary regular approaches me and utters those famous words, 'That's old Charlie's seat.' This is the hint for me to move. Just one seat along will do. Everyone knows you don't sit in the place of a regular, especially an Old Boy. But, to be honest, the first time this happened I was feeling a bit argumentative:

'That's okay, I'll shift when he gets here,' I said.

'Sorry, you'll have to move now, he gets here at seven.'

'But that's 20 minutes away,' I reminded the barman. 'Is he likely to be early?'

'No. He's here at seven on the dot every night,' I was assured by the barman with no logic.

I concluded he didn't like a warm barstool and moved half a metre along the bar. I never did see Charlie; I had finished my beer and gone before he arrived. I will return one day at five to seven and loiter beside (but most definitely not sit on) his stool.

Other pub characters

An Old Boy clinging to his favourite seat is just one of the classic characters in a pub. You know how to treat him (give him his seat). But there are other characters and you should know how to treat them too.

The blokes at the bar

Strangers should approach with caution. Women going up to the bar should prepare themselves for the offer, 'Squeeze in here, darling?' Bet you can't resist, eh?

The women at the bar

Strangers should approach with extreme caution. As the night progresses, men should prepare themselves for bottom pinching.

The amateur philosopher

This guy knows everything. The weather patterns in the Cayman Islands, the price of milk in Asda, how to cook a chicken tikka masala like the local tandoori – he simply knows everything. Most importantly though, he has also done everything everyone else has done, and more. Let's call him the been-there-done-that guy. The sensible rule is to avoid him. However, this would mean missing out on a lot of fun. Instead, occasionally engage him, raising the stakes in the conversation so that your own claims get more and more ridiculous; in other words, play him at his own game. He will not be able to resist raising the stakes, and to the amusement of everyone listening, he will soon be claiming all sorts of rubbish. You have swum with penguins in South Africa, he will have swum with Great Whites off the Barrier Reef, you took a trip in a helicopter, he will have a pilot's licence. Just be careful not to play the game too often or everyone will think you are his friend.

The drinking couple

This is the couple that refuse to leave each other's sides. The woman can sometimes be given honorary status with the boys at the bar, who all love it because she buys her round but only drinks halves. The rule is to talk to this couple as if they are just one person. Always refer to them with joint names (Bill'n'Mary, Christine'n'Dave, etc.) and assume they hold the same views on everything. This last rule falls away after three drinks when the couple will start arguing. If you must take sides, make sure you choose the one whose turn it is to get the beers in.

The canoodling couple

Just leave them alone in the corner. The odd comment along the lines of 'Get a room' or 'Would you like a groundsheet?' is allowed if you know them. Staring as he fondles her under her jumper is not allowed (use the mirror behind the bar).

The suit

This is the guy on the way home from work. Approach him for a chat if he is smiling (he has got a pay rise, sealed a deal or his boss is away). Leave him alone if he has a cloud over his head, is reading a work document or staring into his pint, as there could be all sorts of reasons for this behaviour and, frankly, you don't want to know what they are.

Mr Grumpy

Usually found with his head in a newspaper. Leave him alone. The only person who can approach Mr Grumpy is the amateur philosopher; they will get on okay because Mr Grumpy is actually just a shy amateur philosopher. They will carry on a grumpy, halting conversation with each other while furtively stealing glances at the canoodling couple. (Would someone please tell them about the mirror?)

The joker

This is the perennially happy regular who refuses to let anything get him down, at least in public. He is the flip side of Mr Grumpy but probably even more irritating. Rule one: try not to catch his eye or he will start telling you jokes. Rule two: keep a perma-smile on your face when he is around or he will adopt you as his pet project to make happy. You know all is lost when he says, 'Cheer up, it can't be that bad mate.' At this stage, find another place to drink.

'Just leave the canoodling couple alone in the corner. Staring as he fondles her under her jumper is not allowed (use the mirror behind the bar).'

The lone woman

If she is alone for more than five minutes she is either mad or after a man. Or, heaven forbid, she might actually have popped in for a quiet drink like all the lone men in the pub.

The youngsters

These pub Bambis enter in a daze as if it is their first time away from their mothers (which it might be), dawdle at the entrance and discuss what they are going to drink before gingerly approaching the bar. Then they order and pay for their own drinks one at a time, scrabbling around in their wallets and purses for loose change. Sometimes they even ask what certain drinks cost and adjust their order accordingly. They are then routinely humiliated as the bar staff ask for ID. They have broken so many rules of the pub in so few seconds that they would normally be ostracised forever. However, as they are the pub regulars of tomorrow, regulars should keep quiet and not embarrass them further. We were all like that once.

WHERE TO SIT?

*The bar, the table,
the beer garden?*

We saw in the previous chapter that one place you can't sit in a pub is in an Old Boy's favourite seat. But that doesn't mean you don't still have an amazing array of options open to you – the bar, the tables, the beer garden … However, it is important early on in your pub career that you choose what sort of person you are and stick to it. We can't have people wandering all over the pub or we won't know where we are, will we? So, choose early on if you are a bar person or a table person, a public bar person or a lounge bar person (you must be over 35 for the last bit to make sense. It harks back to the days before the class system had been crushed and people such as builders and bankers had to be kept apart because one was considered 'better' than the other. Yes, yes I know builders are considered better than bankers now … oh, just ask your dad).

Now, there are a few exceptions to the overriding stick-to-where-you-are-sitting rule:

☞ Seasonal. Clearly, with our weather no one can be a beer garden person all year round (or for even more than two weeks), so you are allowed a seasonal change if you like the garden.

☞ Special Event. For instance, if you are a bar person you are allowed to sit at a table if you bring your mum in for Sunday lunch. However, you must not linger any longer than is absolutely necessary at the table. This means you must only sit down as the food is served and leap straight back up the minute the meal is finished and return to your friends.

So just where can you sit/stand in a pub?

Standing at the bar

This is the chosen spot for all those who purport to be pub professionals. The rule of one hand on the bar and one hand on your glass must be maintained at all times. You are allowed the odd movement to avoid seizing up (landlords promote this as ambulances disturb the other customers), but you must not take part in any stretch that looks remotely athletic. If one of the bar drinkers does look athletic, the fat bloke is allowed to say, 'The only exercise I need is this', as he raises his glass to his lips. It is obligatory for all members of the group to laugh as if it is the first time they have heard this joke and to side with the fat bloke even though he will probably drop down dead of a heart attack in a few years. A well-worn joke (if well-timed) beats health any day of the week.

On a stool at the bar

You must be an old man or a woman. Even if you have had a hard day and you are exhausted, if you are under 50 you are not allowed to sit at the bar without first announcing, 'Blimey, I'm knackered,

I need a sit down.' This absolves you of all accusations of being soft and gives you a 15-minute rest before you will be questioned.

On a stool at a tall table

Bar standers can move here (after complaining) if the bar is full. Tall tables should be considered New Towns – just about bearable if the real place you want to be is already full. If the bar still has space then tall tables should only be used as beer perches if you are playing darts or watching the football and the bar is out of reach.

On a chair at a table

You can sit here if you are a couple or old. If you are young, you can sit here if you order food (but only if you really must, what's wrong with the bar?) or if you are playing cards. In all other cases tables should only be considered as things to fill up the gaps between the bar and the walls.

It is heart-warming to see that the giant modern pubs have done away with tables, a move that allows large numbers of people to feel like they are standing at the bar even though they may in fact be metres away. When standing awkwardly in the middle of nowhere in one of those places, don't make the mistake of thinking that the owners have removed the tables as a way of cramming people in and maximising profits. Heaven forbid! No, they have of course realised that choosing where to sit is a minefield and have simply removed that worry, the thoughtful bunch.

I have to say, if I wanted to sit on a couch I would stay at home. But each to their own. There's a pub near me with couches, cushions and big comfy chairs. When I go in there it reminds me of some years ago when I was on holiday in a small Indian town looking for a bar that was showing the cricket. I soon found one and asked the owner sitting outside if he had the cricket on. He duly showed me to a very nice armchair where I settled down to enjoy the game. It was only when I asked for a beer that I realized it was not in fact a bar but his house. Hmm. Use armchairs and couches at home only.

On a bench in the beer garden

Use the beer garden in the summer only, but remember to wear a sunhat, use lots of suncream and don't forget that you will get pissed quicker – this may seem a little overzealous of me on the health and safety advice, but believe me you'll be thanking me when you're happily enjoying the evening sun going down but your mate is throwing up from sunstroke and/or providing you with your own personal heater from his bright red burning face.

The only exceptions to this summer rule are if you smoke (you are allowed to pop out for a puff) or if it is snowing. When it is snowing you are allowed to go out and have a snowball fight. The flat top of the trestle tables makes it easy to gather up the snow (just a little tip for you).

Standing in an awkward place that just irritates everyone

Now, with all the options I've listed above, you'd think there was a happy place for everyone in a pub. But no, even with the bar, the stand-up tables, the sit-down tables and the beer garden, some people are still not happy. This merry bunch choose to stand in the most awkward place they can find: right by the toilet doors, in front of the telly, at the narrowest part of the bar, anywhere in fact where they can piss the rest of us off. Strangely, as you try to squeeze past them they even get annoyed. There are three ways to deal with people like this.

- ☞ Politely point out that where they are standing is making life difficult for everyone and ask if they would mind moving a bit. Unfortunately, this is far too simple a solution for us British as it involves not being embarrassed to talk to strangers, so it's more likely that the following methods will be used.

- ☞ Brush past them (with increased levels of huffing and grunting) in the hope that they will get the point.

- ☞ Wait until Big John eventually gets fed up and threatens to knock them out if they don't move.

Of course, none of the above applies if it is a group of attractive women blocking the way.

'FANCY A GAME OF DARTS, MATE?'

Pub games, teams and quizzes

The Pub Quiz

Quiz nights have been ruined by mobile phones. Even my mother's at it, texting me to find out the price of a first-class stamp at five past ten at night. Why the hell does she want to know that I wonder, before realizing she is probably stuck on question 18 in the Tuesday night quiz down the pub. So, let's start with the rules right here:

☞ Teams should comprise one person who answers nearly all the questions, one who thinks hard and chips in with a couple of answers, one who collects the beer and crisps and one who just sits there dreaming of the day when he will know an answer nobody else does.

☞ All-women teams will need at least one man to 'do sport'.

The team name must be hugely funny to the group who chose it (who are allowed to giggle if is slightly rude) but make absolutely no sense to anyone else in the pub. If possible, it should be offensively topical (such as '[insert name of recently deceased celebrity]'s pension fund') so the quizmaster feels slightly sheepish reading it out. Also, remember there will always be one team who still think 'Norfolk in Chance' is the wittiest team name ever.

The quizmaster must really believe he is a TV show host even if there are only three teams.

You should whisper really loudly when discussing the possible answers so half the pub can hear. And when you don't know the answer, whisper even more loudly the incorrect answer just to flummox the rest of the teams.

☞ When you have no clue whatsoever on a question, just listen to the loud (but not overly loud) whispers from the surrounding tables.

☞ The winners must come from the group congregating round the bar. This is because, by virtue of being at the bar, they are allowed to be helped by bar staff, people coming up for drinks and everyone else in the pub who is not officially playing. They should also feel slightly embarrassed if they receive answers from more than 20 different people, but this is not a hard-and-fast rule.

☞ When two or more teams have the same final score, there will be a tie-breaker. This is the best bit of a pub quiz because after two hours of questioning, one member of each team will have to stand up at the front and risk losing the grand prize of a six-pack of Carlsberg, a peaked cap and a T-shirt all because he can't remember who wrote 'Waltzing Matilda' (no, I'm not telling you, go and look it up you lazy thing). Instead, his team has to settle for one Carlsberg bottle opener between six of them and he will have to make the walk of shame back through the pub. Life's a bitch.

Real pub games

Quizzes though, let's be honest, aren't up there with real pub games. Real pub games are pool and darts, while in a few places these are joined by bar billiards, dominoes and cards. When it comes to the main two you can be an occasional 'just for fun' player or a 'league' player. You will sometimes hear the term 'super

10 of the Best Quiz Team Names

1. Hung Like a Giraffe
2. Quiz Team Aguilera
3. Quiz Akabusi
4. The Scrambled Eggheads
5. I'm Late and I'm On My Own
6. Crouching Woman, Hidden Cucumber
7. 42 (The Answer to the Universe)
8. Simple Minds
9. Barman, a Round of Drinks for This Team From Me
10. Clitoris Allsorts

league' player, often in hushed tones of reverence. This does not mean the league is more fun (as in 'super' in the *Famous Five* books) it just means it is a better level or the player can actually be bothered to travel miles on a rainy Wednesday night for a game of darts or pool. Don't ask, it beats me too.

If you are an occasional player you are:

☞ Allowed to lose and not care

☞ Allowed to try trick shots and laugh when the ball falls off the table (it's not advisable to laugh when the cue ball/dart hits the big bloke sitting at the corner table, however)

☞ Allowed to say you could play in the league but can't be bothered.

If you are a league player you are:

☞ Allowed to have your own cue/darts, and even keep them behind the bar. Retrieving these personal items must be done with a flourish if there are strangers in the bar, just so they know how good you (think) you are. It is acceptable to pause at the bar until one of the regulars tells the strangers, 'He's a league player you know.' The stranger is expected to nod in appreciation and is not expected to say, 'So what?'

☞ Allowed to pretend you were not playing your 'best game' if you lose to an occasional player.

There are certain words and phrases you must use during every game of pool:

☞ 'Hustler'. This can be used after a player you don't know plays a good shot, while ignoring the actual meaning of the word hustle. If she was really hustling you she would hardly show how good she was, would she?

☞ 'You've played this game before'. Again, used following any good shot. Resist the temptation to respond, 'Of course I bloody have or I wouldn't be able to cut it into the centre pocket like that would I you numpty?'

☞ 'Lucky bugger'. Can be applied to any good shot as begrudging praise or if, indeed, you were a lucky bugger – then you deserve it, you lucky bugger.

☞ 'Sign of a misspent youth'. If your opposite number looks half decent you must attribute it to him spending all his youth playing pool/darts, whereas the truth is that's exactly what most of us did.

Sunday football teams

Any self-respecting pub will have its own football team that will play in Division 12 of the Eastern District Metropolitan League (or similar). In terms of the football pecking order this would be the foundation stone of the pyramid, but hey, it's only a game. The pub's sponsorship of the team can range from just letting them in the pub with their sweaty kit on after the game to fully backing them with kits, after-match sandwiches and trophies. Every so often a well-connected landlord will use free beer and hot food (and possibly, dare we mention, dodgy fivers) to draft in a few good players from other pubs so 'his' team thrashes everyone else in sight. The good players shall be referred to as 'ringers' or 'glory hunters' and shall be regarded with suspicion by everyone else in the pub.

In normal circumstances (i.e. without ringers), however, the regulars should greet each new season with enthusiasm, and a few of them must come to the first couple of games (in August when it is sunny). However, as winter sets in and the team reverts to losing ways, regulars are allowed to simply wait at the pub (where they would be anyway) until the players trudge back with tales of biased referees and six of the opposition's seven goals being offside. Whoever managed to score the pub's consolation goal is allowed to embellish facts about the nature of his goal; the distance from which the ball was struck shall grow in direct proportion to the amount of beer consumed (this is known as the Theory of Relative Drunkenness).

Quiz and fruit machines

No one really wins on these in the long run. Some people say they do, some people are rumoured to, but the only ones who really win are those in possession of that mythical electronic thingy that fiddles the machine (note the pub business denies these exist so just ignore those blokes who pop in at noon, order a Coke and shoot off with the jackpot five minutes later).

I love the honesty of the fruit machine. Somewhere at the top in small writing will be a sticker stating : 'This machine pays out 78 percent.' Don't you just love it? 'Give me a tenner and I'll give you £7.80 back' – now there's an offer you can't refuse. The chance to increase your winnings by gambling on another click of the button is irresistible but judging by the amount of kicks, bangs and 'fucks' flying around, the success rate appears to be quite low.

Quiz machines are best played in a group when drunk. This is because everyone, much to the delight of the machine's owners, can try to outsmart each other by guessing the answer quickly without actually reading the question. At this point, the person who has put the money in is allowed to shout and scream, push everyone aside and demand that he and only he will answer the questions from now on (until he gets stuck).

DON'T TOUCH THE NUTS

Bar snacks and food

Food freebies

There are a few occasions when British pubs hand out food freebies. Free bar tapas is the norm in Madrid, and the occasional bowl of cured biltong is not out of place in downtown Johannesburg, but somehow there's something different about free food in our pubs. It's often unexpected and is therefore usually met with some level of suspicion; it's almost like the customers can't believe their luck. Most even comment when the freebie bowls come out, 'Blimey, never thought we'd see anything for nothing in this place, eh lads?' The fact that every Sunday for the last 17 years, freebies have been wheeled out in that same pub doesn't seem to matter. Good old British embarrassment, you can't beat it. And embarrassment is at the heart of all the rules of Sunday food freebies.

The Rules

☞ You must show a total lack of interest when the food comes out. After all, who wants to look desperate for a free bit of cheese or a roast potato?

☞ When you eventually take a lump of cheese, you must take just one, further emphasizing the fact that you are uninterested.

☞ When other people start tucking in you are allowed to grab two bits of cheese before they all disappear, but be careful not to escalate things by taking too much.

☞ You will, however, feel stupid when someone else comes along and takes the whole lot without a care in the world. It could have been you. Embarrassment sucks, now go and pay 80p for a packet of crisps.

There is an over-rider to all the above:

☞ Don't. Touch. The. Nuts. The bowls of food, naturally, are communal. This means that if they're the type of food that requires scooping to pick up (e.g. nuts), then there will have been a lot of fingers all over the food you're about to eat. (I suggest you refer to the chapter on toilets and the bit on not washing hands and weigh up your chances of getting a horrible disease.)

So, I propose a new rule:

☞ Be the first to dip your fingers into the bowl, sod the embarrassment, take a bloody great handful and never touch the bowl again 'til next Sunday.

Occasions other than Sunday when you can get free food are:

☞ After work. Some pubs put out some basic snacks, such as peanuts, for a short burst to catch the after-work crowd. Most people (grumpy buggers) believe it's just to make your mouth salty so you order more drinks. Maybe it is, maybe it isn't. Just embrace the moment and order another pint to get rid of the salty taste. At least you've got a decent excuse for staying for more than one when you get home.

☞ When the pub darts/pool team play. The pub will put on complimentary sandwiches and sausage rolls. You want a free sandwich? Simply linger around the edges of the match and ask them how they are getting on as if you actually give a shit. A ham sandwich is your reward; maybe even a sausage roll if they are winning.

☞ When your mate buys a packet of something from behind the bar. It is obligatory for anyone buying a packet of crisps or peanuts (not a pickled egg) to share the goods. How much to take? You have to weigh up how long it is until you're going to buy something because it's tit-for-tat when it comes to taking other mates' crisps. So, if your purchase is a long way off, go ahead and gorge.

Buying snacks

The first thing to remember when ordering crisps, which would probably account for about 83 per cent of all snacks sold in a pub if a survey was ever done, is to always ask the barmaid to reel off the full list of what is on offer. When she has finished reading out all 22 flavours, '… smokey bacon, sea salt, turkey and stuffing, builder's breakfast …', simply choose cheese and onion. It is your right as a customer to hear the full list of flavours read out, so do not be deterred by the mounting anger of either the staff or the queue of people waiting to be served.

The other, lesser-eaten snacks have their own rules that must be followed.

Peanuts

Like all snacks, peanuts must be shared in the most unhygienic way possible by everyone at the bar (i.e., let them all dip their fingers in the packet). The good thing with peanuts is that the packet is so small the first packet disappears to your mates and you can just order another packet, which you are now permitted to eat yourself.

Not so long ago, as every man knows, the primary reason for buying peanuts was that the cardboard backing they hung on had a photo of a woman in a bikini and each purchase revealed a bit more of the photo. The bar staff were permitted to tease customers by plucking the packets from the edges, leaving her nicest bits covered until the last few packets were sold. It wasn't a rule that the person who bought the last packet kept the image, but it should

have been. Recently, in the spirit of political correctness, the bikini girl has been replaced by witty slogans such as 'This product contains nuts'. Again, it's not a rule that the slogans (amusing though they are) should be ditched for the girl, but it should be.

Pork scratchings

Anyone who doesn't like them (and let's admit it, they are a love-'em-or-hate-'em snack) must exclaim, 'Urgh, how can you eat those?!' whenever anyone orders a packet. The person who likes them is then, in turn, permitted to shove a pig rind under the nose of everyone to try to convert them. Naturally, religious jokes abound at this point.

Pickled eggs

The love-'em-or-hate-'em rule applies here too, and those who do like them can flaunt their culinary bravado while others wince. However, there is also an allowed curiosity rule, i.e., you may ask the bar staff if 'anyone actually eats those things'. (The fact that they are sitting there in a jar might be the clue, I should add.)

Pepperami, sausage rolls, etc.

If you are this hungry you should go to the chip shop.

Top 5 Pub Snacks

1. Crisps: in a recent and thorough survey, every single person who had ever entered a pub had bought a packet of crisps at some point. Except one or two.
2. Pickled eggs: these must have the date of the pickling on the jar. Check, because you *really* don't want to eat an egg that's older than your teeth.
3. Pickled egg in a bag of crisps: trust me, this is lovely. And, best of all, it stops people eating your crisps.
4. Cheese and onion rolls: always best on a Saturday morning and almost always made by a barmaid named Carol.
5. Peanuts: you have read the title of this book, right?

Pub meals

There are, of course, proper meals to be had in pubs. In fact, you'd be hard pressed to find a pub today that doesn't at least offer bangers and mash or burger and chips. Ordering a pub meal makes sense for two reasons.

☞ You can now go to the pub on Mother's Day without feeling guilty.

☞ You can now go to the pub on your girlfriend's birthday without feeling guilty.

It is accepted wisdom that many pubs only survive thanks to their food trade and for that at least we should applaud the chefs (or the people who warm up the pre-packed meals). I am, however, delighted that certain rules have been applied to eating in pubs to stop the customers actually thinking these places exist for the food.

☞ Under no circumstances can anyone receive table service. You need to know where you are sitting, order at the bar and pay in advance McDonald's style (but pay restaurant prices).

☞ Items on the menu cannot be swapped – if it says chips then chips it is, no mashed potato allowed.

☞ It is forbidden for staff to put cutlery or sauces on the table the customer is using. These must all be stored as far away as possible and, frankly, such things should be considered the customers' problem anyway.

'THIS IS MY GAFF!'

The guv'nor and bar staff

Guv'nors

A good guv'nor can get you popping into a pub for a chat and a beer because you feel welcome, while a bad one can drive you away after one beer, never to return to that pub again. Guv'nors (the man or woman who runs a pub, and not the gangster who comes in and drinks on Fridays) come in many guises. There are landlords/landladies who own or lease the pub (i.e. it is their business), managers who run the pub for the breweries or a boss, and absent landlords who swan in (or come downstairs) and just drink with the regulars and direct the bar staff. But, basically guv'nors boil down to two types.

The friendly guv'nor

It is almost odd that a guv'nor should have to be identified as friendly, isn't it? After all, who would take on a job that includes dealing with people who have come to spend their money in their (entertainment) business and not be friendly? But friendly should not be taken for granted. If you find a pub with a friendly landlord, keep drinking in it. A friendly guv'nor can be spotted because he:

☞ Greets you when you come into the pub (whether or not you are a regular)

☞ Remembers what you drink after a few visits

- Will not say, 'Bloody hell mate, your bird has got a great backside'

- Chats to you when it is quiet

- Leaves you alone when you are reading a newspaper/ grappling with a Sudoku

An exceptionally friendly guv'nor will:

- Actually introduce you to other people in the pub

- Buy you a drink

- Remember your name

The grumpy guv'nor

Strangely, this lot are in the majority. So let me ask them all right now, on behalf of all the drinkers in the world who are too polite to say it: 'What are you doing in the pub business? Yes, you, sitting at the end of the bar with a long face because I have dared to disturb your lunch and ask for a beer. Did I know it was your lunchtime? No I didn't. But clearly everyone else within 20 miles of this place does because this pub of yours is bloody empty. Shall I remind you what that means? It means you will not be eating lunch at all soon because you won't have a job/business you miserable old git.' Ahhhhhh, that feels better. Grumpy landlords are identified by:

☞ Being grumpy

☞ Being grumpy in an empty pub

Bar staff

Bar staff are the lifeblood of the pub industry so it's odd that they should be paid so badly. As if serving you beer every day was not enough, they also act as friends, counsellors, objects of your Barbara Windsor-type fantasies, organisers of your taxis and takeaways, and wipers of your tears when your girlfriend leaves you. All in all, three cheers for bar staff, we love you all. Except this first lot.

The grumpy ones

This group have somehow learnt from grumpy bosses that this is how to do it. They constantly moan about the things they are actually paid to do, tell people to keep the noise down if there is the merest hint of fun emerging from a group, and watch the clock throughout their shift so all the drinkers feel uncomfortable. The question on everyone's lips (but rarely verbalised) is: 'Why exactly are you working in a pub?'

The enthusiastic beginner

Working behind a bar is a bit like being on stage, and the first time is nerve-racking. Think of all those issues relating to the first day in a new job but with everyone watching you. Newbies to the bar trade (usually students, people who have just lost their job or stayed-at-home-too-long mums trying to meet people) are generally:

☛ Wide-eyed

☛ Gullible to all jokes because they are concentrating on where everything is

☛ Slow

However, it only takes a few weeks before newbies are telling you to 'sod off' like the rest of the bar staff and will have Old Charlie's beer ready for him before he's even settled into his favourite seat.

The old hand

Been there, done it. Friendly, but not too friendly, and always efficient. Like a friendly landlord, find a pub with an old hand working in it and drink in it. You will get the drink you want, the correct change and all delivered with a smile and respect (grumpy bar staff please take note). I once sat quietly on a particularly busy Saturday night in my local as the queues, dirty glasses and customer tetchiness started to build up due to a couple of newbies struggling. Viv, a particularly good old hand, who was enjoying a night with friends on the other side of the bar, watched in horror. Ten minutes later she'd collected all the glasses around the pub, filled the dishwasher and reduced the queue to zero. As I said earlier, they are not paid enough.

The tourist guide

Clearly in the wrong job, the tourist-guide barman serves you a beer then starts to tell you about the local delights of the area. This is all well and good if you are in an area that is interesting, but not if you are in Leicester.

The Aussie/Kiwi

Certainly not lacking in confidence, the Aussie (on a backpacking trip, of course) will give as good as he gets. They will all (without exception) tell you that no one drinks Foster's in Australia and they will have been to more places in the UK and the rest of Europe in the last six months than most of the bar regulars have visited in their lives. The Kiwi is more of the same, but with a bit less front.

The Pole/Lithuanian/Estonian

Young, good looking and staffing the pubs British locals can't be arsed to worked in. You'll know them by their accents, which are either Polish, Lithuanian or Estonian strangely enough. Unlike the Australians, they are here to make money rather than see Cambridge or Amsterdam, but there's a good chance they'll have been to Prague.

'The tourist-guide barman . . . is all well and good if you are in an area that is interesting, but not if you are in Leicester.'

'FREE BEER TOMORROW'

The baffling world of pub style

Pub Types

Pubs all have their own character, but sometime way back in the 1940s or '50s there must have been an MP with a business making heavy, red, chintzy wallpaper and curtains, and dark-wood bar tops, and thus it was duly made law that (nearly) all pubs should be obliged to use these items. Pubs come in the following guises:

The old-style traditional pub

This is what the tourists come to see, a good old British pub as it should be. Dark, a well-worn bar, red wallpaper and chintz curtains, as per the above. Yellowing smoke stains should still remain on the ceiling as homage to the days when smoking was allowed. There should be little nooks for, er, nooky, I suppose. Bar stools will be covered with leftover red material and there shall be hooks under the bar so you can hang your coat or handbag. The flooring can be either wooden floorboards or a carpet that has seen better days (just after the War). Charlie (*see* page 42) will be sitting at the bar, although there is some discussion as to whether he is part of the decor or not.

The refurb

The same as above but cleaner. Charlie is unlikely to return until the cobwebs have, as he doesn't like change.

The modern

These are designed for people who don't like the red wallpaper or curtains. As such, they don't look like real pubs at all.

JD Wetherspoons

These must remind you of an aircraft hangar, except you'll be able to get cheap food and beer, which, as far as I know, you can't find in a real aircraft hangar.

Wine bars

These probably have shares in Ikea because they all look like Scandinavian showhouses.

Traditional Pub Accessories

To be considered a real British pub, however, all the following items must be found somewhere:

Foreign notes and coins on the wall

These are to be stuck to the wall with Blu-Tack and look as tatty as possible in as short a time as possible. They are to display the worldliness of the clientele who donate them to the pub when they return from holiday. Backpackers are the most sought-after customers as they will return with all sorts of strange Polish zlotys, Venezuelan bolivars and Zambian kwachas for the wall. Top of the pecking order are notes from places where the majority of the customers are unlikely to visit (i.e. anywhere except Spain, Greece and France). The type of notes on the wall act as a barometer for the bar's knowledge of geography.

'Burkina Faso, that's in South America, isn't it Bill?'

'Don't be silly, there's an African guy's picture on the note.'

'I'm not sure about that, he looks Asian to me.'

'No, no, he's got a big nose.'

At this point someone else who is listening in horror can point out that comments about stereotypes, especially body parts is not EC (Ethnologically Correct) and the conversation must move to safer geographical waters, such as Denmark.

A newspaper cutting

Someone who goes in the pub, someone who once went in the pub, someone who is related to someone who goes in the pub or who once went in the pub, someone who someone knows or has heard of, or at a push someone who lives in the area, will have appeared in a newspaper. This cutting should be proudly displayed in the pub. Its purpose is to show newcomers to the place that someone who goes in the pub, someone who once went in the pub, someone who is related to someone who goes in the pub or who once went in the pub, someone who someone knows or has heard of, or, at a push, someone who lives in the area has appeared in a newspaper.

A 'funny' sign

There are only two of these apparently. The most common is 'Free Beer Tomorrow', and the other, used presumably when the first choice is sold out, is 'Free beer to everyone over 80 (if accompanied by both parents)'. If anyone ever comments on the sign and laughs you should not look astonished (bless him), but from thereon in you should look for other signs of alien life in the pub.

10 Favourite Pub Signs

1. '24 Hours in a Day, 24 Beers in a Case – Coincidence?'
2. 'Beer: Helping Ugly People Have Sex Since 1862'
3. 'Avoid Hangovers: Stay Drunk!'
4. 'When I Read About the Evils of Drinking, I Gave Up Reading'
5. 'I'm Not as Think as You Drunk I Am'
6. 'Save Water, Drink Beer!'
7. 'I'm Not An Alcoholic, I'm A Drunk. Alcoholics Go To Meetings.'
8. 'If I Gave a Crap, You Would Be the First Person I Gave It To'
9. 'Why Be Difficult When With Just a Little Effort You Can Be Impossible?'
10. 'Beauty Lies in the Hands of the Beer Holder'

Photos of locals in various states of undress, fancy dress and drunkenness

These are to show what a fun pub you are in, even though every time you go in it's just you and the Old Boy in the corner. The photos on the pub wall, taken on New Year's Eve or the annual karaoke night, must include one of the male regulars dressed as a woman, a couple (who aren't a couple) kissing, a group of girls showing their cleavage, someone drunk and asleep, and an old bloke staring at the camera looking bemused.

'The photos on the pub wall must include one of the male regulars dressed as a woman, someone drunk and asleep, and an old bloke staring at the camera looking bemused.'

Some evidence of community

A good pub must be like your family, that's an absolute rule of a good pub. If you've got no family, you go to the pub; if you've got no wife, you go to the pub; if you've got no friends, you go to the pub (in fact even if you have got a family, wife and friends you still go to the pub, but that's besides the point). Therefore, as well as selling beer and food and supplying entertainment, a pub is obliged to organise sporting events (golf society, football team), a chance to gamble (Lottery bonus ball), and travel trips (day out to Hastings or horse racing in York). All these events can be pinned to the informal community notice board along with the phone number of a man with a van, someone else who will do any odd job for cash (except electrical work), the local taxi firm and the offer of babysitting at £6 an hour from Mary's teenage daughter (references available). Photos of pub teams dating back to the '80s are always good – if only to prove that Guinness Tom had hair once upon a time.

'Events can be pinned to the noticeboard along with someone who will do any odd job for cash (except electrical work).'

A collection bottle

As there is no culture of tipping bar staff in Britain (heaven forbid), unlike in many other countries, an oversized charity bottle is available for all loose change. The charity supported must have some significance to one of the regulars or the staff. If you walk more than three steps from the bar and have not collected your change you are obliged to point to the bottle, indicating to the barman where your change should go. This should be done with a casual flourish to show how generous you are. The letter from the charity ('Thank you to everyone in the Holly Bush for raising £53.76 for the Support Children's Fund last year') must be stuck next to the bottle to show everyone their change was actually sent off to the charity and not added to the staff Christmas party fund.

'THIS ONE'S FOR LOUISE'

Music in pubs

Jukeboxes

These were invented for pub managers really. Not only do we, the customers, have to pay for our food and drink but we also have to cough up for the pub's entertainment. Brilliant. But the worst bit is that you don't even know if you'll hear the songs you put on because when it's really busy you have no idea how many tracks are programmed in the machine already. The rule is just to wait patiently then triumphantly exclaim, 'This is my one!' Sad, but true.

The Basic Rules

In a quiet pub everyone sits there analysing your choices and working out what sort of person you are based on what music you put on the jukebox; it's the equivalent of taking your CD collection down the pub and letting everyone sift through it. So, follow these simple rules:

☞ If you are a man do not put anything soppy on.

☞ If you are the only woman in the pub do not put anything on with the word 'sex' in it. And, whatever mood you are in, don't punch in Kylie's 'I Should Be So Lucky' – they don't need encouraging.

☞ If the pub is full of skinheads do not put Bob Marley on, unless you are right by the door and can make a dash for it.

☞ If the jukebox has been playing uptempo hits to an appreciative audience all night, it's probably not the best time to introduce an obscure Leonard Cohen album track, even if it is your favourite.

Jukeboxes, especially today's electronic versions, have literally thousands of songs on them. It's all a bit of a waste really because most pubs just play the same old songs over and over again (*see* lists below). Anyone who disagrees should send their own lists, together with a £50 note, to the publisher's address (please mark it for my attention).

Sing-songs

Although you may still find an old-style sing-song with renditions of 'Roll Out the Barrel' in the East End, you're likely to have to look long and hard. Today's sing-songs, although equally as drunken, tend to be single-sex group bonding events. As alcohol kicks in and the group on a boys'/girls' night out feels the need to show some emotion, a sing-song is what is needed. This is because music and singing along to it removes the no-touching-a-person-of-the-same-sex-if-you-are-a-hetero rule. There is a period of grace at the end of the song where the group or members of it are allowed a stronger hug (almost a celebration of getting-through-it-without-collapsing hug), but they must withdraw soon after – it's a bit like coming out of hypnosis and finding yourself in an awkward situation.

Girls' (women are 'girls' in pubs when it comes to groups and singing) sing-song choices:

☞ 'I Will Survive' by Gloria Gaynor (also a big choice among the gay crowd)

☞ 'Don't Cha' ('wish your girlfriend was hot like me') by Pussycat Dolls (sung with pouting lips, boobs pushed out and to an adoring male audience, i.e. anyone in the pub)

☞ 'It's Raining Men' by the Weather Girls (another gay-crowd favourite)

☞ 'Angels' by Robbie Williams (because all women are, of course)

Boys' (same story as above) sing-song choices:

☞ 'Another One Bites the Dust' by Queen (apart from the macho edge to the words, this track is great because it has two parts to it, allowing two groups to sing a part each and make it sound like they know what they are doing)

☞ 'Ring of Fire' by Johnny Cash (need only sing the title and the did-did-did-der-der-der bit)

☞ 'Wild Rover' (accompanied by loud foot stomping at the relevant point)

☞ 'Up Up and Away' by Fifth Dimension (anyone can sing this)

☞ 'Stand By Me' by Ben E. King (staring into another man's eyes is permitted if ironic)

Dancing

A special skill of many pubs is in how they transform themselves from quiet boozers to discos. Dancing is only allowed to start after ten (or nine on weekends), which is about the time it takes for everyone to be drunk enough. Dancing is never allowed if anyone is still playing dominoes. Just think about it. Could you shake your thang if someone else was playing dominoes? The most popular dancing songs are:

☞ 'Come on Eileen' by Dexy's Midnight Runners (purely for that mad few seconds in the middle of the song when everyone is permitted to go bonkers and then wonder why they are not as good at it as they were at the school disco 25 years ago)

☞ 'You Can't Hurry Love' by Phil Collins (come on, anyone can dance to this, and there is always the original Supremes version to talk about afterwards)

☞ 'Dancing Queen' by Abba (for the girls and the gay crowd)

Staring into your glass songs

In keeping with the community aspect of pubs, while you would normally never discuss what you paid for a pot of creosote, it is perfectly acceptable to discuss all aspects of your love life and wallow in the misery of a lost love/divorce in front of the entire pub. You are allowed to listen to these songs for two days following a break-up, after which the sympathy stops and Madness must be back on the jukebox.

☞ 'When Will I See You Again?' by The Three Degrees (tears are permitted as long as you don't blub)

☞ 'Yesterday' by The Beatles (all your troubles will be far away by the end of the fifth pint, don't worry)

☞ 'When a Man Loves a Woman' by Percy Sledge (heads must slump almost into the beer at the start of Percy's wailing)

☞ 'Release Me' by Englebert Humperdinck (a giveaway as to the reason for the break-up)

☞ 'Suspicious Minds' by Elvis Presley (*see* above)

Songs to sing to the barmaid

There is a peculiar leap in confidence from (usually reserved) men who suddenly spring into action and serenade the barmaid when drunk. Chosen songs should always have some backing lyrics (the 'ooo's of The Righteous Brothers' tracks make them a classic for this) or an easy chorus so a group of men can do the singing. The men might be drunk but there is no way anyone would do this without the support of friends.

- ☞ 'You've Lost that Loving Feeling' by The Righteous Brothers (every man must sing this to a barmaid at least once in his life, even if he just mouths the words while looking at her; it's a rite of passage)

- ☞ 'Baby I Need Your Loving' by Johnny Rivers (did he actually write this for drunks to serenade barmaids with?)

- ☞ 'My Girl' by The Temptations (if you've just started going out with her)

- ☞ 'Can't Take My Eyes Off You' by Frankie Valli (sing it like an old crooner for maximum effect)

- ☞ 'Always on My Mind' by Elvis (the lyrics are a bit sad but they work nonetheless)

Songs to be played every night in the traditional boozer

Ageing wannabe rock stars are permitted to play air guitar and mime without undue laughter to the following:

- ☞ 'A Whiter Shade of Pale' by Procol Harum (long, long track for frustrated old drinkers who'd rather be a rock star)

- ☞ 'Stairway to Heaven' by Led Zeppelin (ditto)

☞ 'Bohemian Rhapsody' by Queen (ditto)

☞ 'Layla' by Eric Clapton (ditto)

☞ 'All Right Now' by Free (ditto)

Songs to be played every night in a slightly younger boozer

☞ 'Rehab' by Amy Winehouse (ironically sung the loudest by those who are the most pissed)

☞ 'Ruby' by Kaiser Chiefs (the modern sing-song track)

☞ 'Fix Up, Look Sharp' by Dizzee Rascal (would it be fair to say that when Nottingham starts dancing to rap it's completely lost its edge?)

☞ 'I Kissed a Girl' by Katy Perry (wouldn't have anything to do with the lesbian thing would it?)

☞ 'Human' by The Killers (the easy way to ask someone to dance – 'are we human or are we dancers?')

'EXCUSE ME MATE, I CAN'T SEE THE GAME'

Pubs and sport

In England and Scotland, football must be on the pub's TV at all times except in the following instances:

☞ When the Ashes is on (on in England if things are going well and on in Scotland if they're not)

☞ For nine minutes while the Grand National is being run, especially if the pub regulars have a bet on

☞ For 18 minutes while the University Boat Race is on (applies only to Oxford and Cambridge and pubs where alumni drink)

☞ During Wimbledon until the last British player is knocked out (in the old days this meant about two days, but Tim

Henman and Andy Murray have prolonged the tennis into week two in recent years)

☞ When it's karaoke night (on quiz night the sound on the TV can be turned down)

In Wales, substitute 'football' for 'rugby'.

In pubs where there is more than one TV, certain other events, such as the Six Nations, British and Irish Lions Test matches and Formula One, can be shown on the crappy TV with poor colour in the corner. The sound must be turned down, though, so as not to disturb the football fans.

So now we have got the minority sports out the way we can concentrate on the rules of watching the football.

☞ When there is a choice of more than one game the one chosen will be Manchester United. The only exception to this rule is in Manchester, where they watch Manchester City.

☞ If Manchester United are not playing and there is a choice, the game shown will be the one the loudmouth at the bar wants, regardless of whether everyone else wants to watch the other game.

☞ If a big match follows the one the loudmouth is watching, this will not be viewed until he has heard the post-match interview with the managers. The rest of the pub is entitled to be as sick as parrots.

⤷ One (or more) of the blokes at the bar will exclaim regularly how they could do better. After three pints they must declare that they could have made it as a professional but they preferred booze and women so gave up aged 18. It is not advisable to ask the dreamer why he gave up £80,000 a week, a Ferrari and a WAG with long legs just so he could spend Sunday afternoons in the Dog and Duck.

⤷ All pub football fans must learn to continue all activities (drinking, ordering beer and roasted peanuts, heading to the toilet, smoking, talking, texting, etc.) without once taking their eyes from the game. Stumbling around and bumping into people like you are a zombie from the 'Walking Dead' is only acceptable during the match. You will be fair game for a smack in the mouth if you do this when the game is not on.

⤷ If you need a piss while the game is on it's best to hold it in. If that's impossible, head for the toilet without taking your eyes off the match. Linger by the door waiting for an interruption in proceedings (injury, corner, etc.) then race in, force it out and race back. If a goal is scored against your team while you are in the toilet you will be to blame. However, you will be lauded as 'lucky' if your team scores. This is not as good as it sounds, because for the rest of the game you will be pushed towards the urinals numerous times in an attempt to bring more luck to your team.

⤷ Anyone who actually goes to the game (they do still exist) is allowed to return to the pub afterwards and explain the finer details of what really happened in the match as if the TV close-ups, the replays and all the analysis were not available.

The TV watchers must defer because it is unfair to argue with someone who paid £50 to see what the rest have enjoyed for nothing.

☛ When England are playing they shall be referred to as 'pathetic', 'crap' and 'lacking passion', regardless of how they are actually playing.

THE TOILETS

The rules of the gents' and ladies'

Chatting in the gents'

While you should never chat to a stranger in Britain when on a train, on a bus, on the street, standing in a queue, in a restaurant, at an airport, when out walking, while in a coffee shop or in a supermarket (in fact, on just about any occasion or in any circumstances), it is perfectly acceptable to launch into conversation when you have your dick in your hand at the urinals. If the English all lived in a gents' toilet we would be the friendliest bunch of people on earth. It generally goes like this:

'Alright mate?'

'Yeah, not so bad.'

At this stage it is obligatory to follow up with a standard joke about the bodily function you are both performing; something along the lines of:

'Better out than in, eh?'

or:

'All that money for a beer and we're getting rid of it already, eh?'

Ho ho ho.

Thankfully, the standard length of a piss doesn't last much longer than the time it takes to utter those words so the conversation rarely goes much further than a brief mention of the match on the TV, the weather or the barmaid's cleavage. And, while the conversation may seem inane, it fulfils the important ice-breaker role which now enables you to continue the conversation with your dick safely tucked away when back at the bar. Many an afternoon or evening has been spent in conversation with a group of strangers only because a brief chit-chat was launched in the urinals.

'Hey John, meet my friends and join us for a pint and a game of darts.'

'How did we meet? Oh we've just been chatting in the gents.'

It is perfectly acceptable to introduce a new friend you have met in the toilets, but not someone you met on the train – that would be downright weird.

However, even though the urinals may seem like a friendly island in a sea of English shyness, be warned – there are some essential rules when striking up a conversation with a fellow 'pisser'. Be sure to follow these to the letter to avoid embarrassment.

☛ You must both have your willies out. To strike up a conversation with a stranger while he has his out and you are fully clothed is not allowed; you must both be disarmed, so to speak. The earliest point to start a conversation is as you are unzipping as this at least shows intent.

☛ Only chance conversations are permitted. Hanging about in the toilets all night, hoping to meet someone for a chat, will get you arrested.

☞ Under no circumstances can you shake hands at the end of the conversation.

☞ Depending on the type of pub you are in, after your piss, you must a) march straight out as if the handbasin does not exist (in a hard pub) or b) lather up your hands with soap and water as if you are about to perform heart surgery (in a poncey pub). Cleanliness seems to have a direct link with hardness and when it comes to appearances or contracting some horrible disease there should be no compromise. Always maintain appearances or you will hear the locals muttering, 'Yeah, I though he was a nice bloke but then I saw him wash his hands.'

☞ There must be a distance of at least one urinal between you and the other bloke if you are to have a conversation. If you chat to someone you are standing next to this will be considered to be a move on him. This rule leads to some interesting cross-conversations along the urinals, with people desperate for a chat, but not allowed to include the bloke standing next to them. Therefore, simply consider the urinal next to you as invisible when it comes to conversations.

☞ The talking rule does not apply to someone who's in a cubicle by the way. While it's ok to chat to someone at the urinal who's got his dick out, it is just downright weird to talk through a door, especially when someone has his trousers round his ankles. And while we are at it: you, yes you with your trousers round your ankles: could you please refrain from using your mobile? We can all hear you and we don't want to.

The urinals

Let's be honest, standing next to a stranger while having a piss is not everyone's idea of fun, but there is one incontrovertible unspoken rule:

☞ DO NOT look at the size of someone else's dick (if, for some reason, you do, it is advisable to walk out of the toilet, straight out of the pub, into your car/taxi/bus and never return to that pub again).

The rest of the rules are complicated, yet understood by everyone.

If there is only one urinal and it is being used:

☞ Use the cubicle

☞ Wait

Under no circumstances do you say 'Oi! Budge up mate, I'm bursting.'

If there are two urinals and both are free:

☞ You can use either one, safe in the knowledge that nobody will stand next to you unless it gets really busy.

☞ Use the cubicle, although this is generally considered a bit namby-pamby. It is better to assert first dibs on the urinals like a man.

If there are two urinals and one is being used:

☞ Use the cubicle

☞ Use the other urinal *only* if the cubicle is busy. Certain people may even opt to wait, uncertain, even at this stage. If you enter a gents' and one urinal is free but someone is still waiting, after a perfunctory nod and grunt it is acceptable to queue jump. Make the most of it, as this is probably the only time in England that queue jumping is allowed. The person waiting will often nod towards the cubicle as if he wants a dump. It is better to admit to needing a dump than to being too shy to piss next to someone else.

If there are three urinals and they are all free:

☞ Always take an end one so the next person to enter the gents' is not forced to stand next to you.

☞ Only take the middle one if you are trying to assert some sort of bravado (e.g. if you are a local wanting to show the rules do not count for you and are daring a new visitor to stand next to you).

If there are three urinals and they are being used:

☞ If one end is being used, take the other end one.

☞ If the end and middle ones are being used it is perfectly acceptable to take the other end one as the standing-next-to-someone-else rule has already been broken.

☞ If the two end ones are taken use a cubicle.

☞ If the two end ones are taken and the cubicle is being used you must use a standard joke along the lines of 'Room for a little one?' to show that you recognise you are about to break the standing-next-to-someone-else rule.

It should also be noted that if you do break the standing-next-to-someone-else rule because you have no choice you lose the right to start a conversation. Look, you can't have everything. And if you break the standing-next-to-someone-else rule when you don't have to and you start a conversation then, er, well, don't worry about that because no one has done that and lived to tell the tale.

Women's toilets

- ☞ Smell nicer then the gents'

- ☞ Are viewed by women as an alternative place for chatting. Hence, women never go to the toilets without a friend.

- ☞ Are a safer option than the gents' if you've convinced your girlfriend to spice up your love life with a little exhibitionism

and want to have sex in the loos. This is because women are more likely to politely ignore what's going on in the cubicle, whereas in the gents' they'll be queuing up for a gander. And it'll probably be quite a lot cleaner.

If drunk, a woman is also allowed to jump the usually long queue at the ladies' by using the gents'. Upon entering, she is expected say 'Don't mind me, boys' in a loud voice, at which time all the men at the urinals are expected to cover their willies, rather than turn round and greet her with open arms.

Breaking the seal

Apparently your bladder can hold something like a pint to a pint and a half. However, after being to the toilet once in an evening, it can only accept two more mouthfuls before you need to go again. This last bit is not exactly scientific but we all know it's true. The phenomenon is commonly known as 'breaking the seal' and has nothing to do with the stinky sea animals that sharks like to eat. Once your seal has been broken, there's no going back; you'll be back and forth all night. There are, however, a few tricks to keep that seal from breaking.

☞ Drink less liquid (hey, I could have been a rocket scientist). Beer drinkers and, even worse, people who drink pints of soft drinks, are usually the first to go.

☞ Stay young forever (old people are up and down as soon as they've had that first slurp).

☞ Sit there until you are absolutely bursting at the seams. You will look like an over-ripe blueberry and put ridiculous strain on your organs, but hey, it'll save you a 15-metre walk to the toilets.

First dates, in particular, are a nightmare. You don't want to be up and down like someone with a problem, but you also don't want to be sipping on a half pint all night or wetting yourself. Just try to hit it off as early as possible in the evening so that the attraction can withstand you jumping up for the sixth time in half an hour, and remember that your date is also squeezing it in. Why do you think so many first dates are so tense?

Number twos

In a pub, if you disappear for more than two minutes you will be greeted with one of the following:

☞ 'Good shit then mate?'

☞ 'Bet you feel lighter now?'

☞ 'We won't be going in there for a while, eh?'

One of these comments, and a variety of others, will be said in an excessively loud voice, so as to alert the whole pub to your recent bowel movements. You see, even though the whole world shits, it is still considered a mildly amusing and embarrassing activity in an English pub. You have four options:

☛ Do it before leaving your house

☛ Hold it in

☛ Make one of the standard jokes yourself before heading off (e.g. 'Just off for a good shit') to show you really don't care

☛ Get in and out within two minutes so you can stroll back into the bar as if you have only been for a piss.

SMOKERS

Standing out in the cold

Smokers have a special bond because they are a persecuted minority. The fact that their minority is 21 per cent of people over the age of 16 (yes, I actually looked that up) makes them a rather large minority. But it's the persecuted bit that binds them together. They, therefore, gather outside (now smoking is banned in pubs) creating a cloud of smoke, and in that cloud they talk about:

- The days when smoking was allowed in pubs

- How pubs smell of sweat and farts now that smoking has been banned

- The penalty that never was in Sunday's match (or should I say Big Game on 'Super Sunday Exclusive' on Sky/ESPN?)

- How nice it is to enjoy a cigarette outside in the July sun

- The cost of cigarettes

- How the weather is turning chilly now it's October

☞ A bloke up the road who can get cheap cigarettes

☞ How cold it is for smokers outside in February

☞ How much tax is on a packet of cigarettes

☞ How the NHS would collapse if it wasn't for the tax paid by smokers

☞ The new barmaid with the see-through top

☞ How 'we' are bound to get hammered by the Chancellor in the Budget

☞ And finally ... a mystical pub in Kent where the landlord has stuck two fingers up to the law by allowing customers to smoke inside. The ashtrays are cut-off Coke cans to confuse the Smoking Police (as if they need to exist in ever-polite law-abiding Britain).

Those of us who don't smoke (79 per cent, I assume) must, in the meantime, get used to conversations ending mid-sentence as smokers realise they're due another. Exactly where mid-sentence this realisation appears depends on the nicotine cravings of the person we are talking to – 'So, I said to Bill, it's about time we ... Be back in a moment, just popping out for a cig.'

Meanwhile, as they wait for their smoking friend to return, the non-smokers talk about:

☞ How pubs smell of sweat and farts now that smoking has been banned

☞ How cold it must be for smokers outside in February

☞ The new barmaid with the see-through top

'NICE RACK, DARLING'

Barmaids and boobs

Not wanting to sound like a scene from a *Carry On* movie or altogether too 1970s, but frankly barmaids and big tits (any-sized tits, actually) are just so 1970s ... and 1980s ... and 1990s ... and 2000s ... and so 2010s, too. There are only two reasons to go to a pub. Forget the football, the dominoes, the banter. Forget everything. It boils down to this:

1. To drink

2. To chat up the barmaid with the big boobs (any-sized boobs)

Sorry, but that's it. The drinking bit is easy, you don't need my help with that. But when it comes to getting a date with a barmaid you should know there are three approaches:

The quiet approach

This is where you chat up the barmaid gently over time and wait for those magic words, 'You're different to the other blokes who come in this pub.' This is not the signal to pounce or look down for a quick peep at her cleavage, but it shows you are getting somewhere (or she thinks you are gay). You can now ask her out casually:

'We should go out for a drink sometime, not in this pub though,'

as if you are Prince Charming saving her from her Thursday night shift. The rules of the quiet approach are that you avoid staring at her boobs and do not join in any so-called banter with your mates that include any combination of the words 'bend', 'tits', 'big' or 'over'.

Getting her number at this stage is particularly challenging as she won't want the rest of the pub to know she is handing it out. Tactics for sneakily handing it over include:

☞ Writing her number on a newspaper, then asking you if you know the answer to six across.

☞ Punching her number into her phone then pretending to show you something on YouTube.

☞ Jotting down her number on the taxi firm's business card and exclaiming (a bit too loudly), 'Here's the taxi number you wanted Dave.'

None of these tricks actually fool anyone but it's still not a good idea to head back to your mates, waving the piece of paper around and cheering.

The completely brazen approach

Chat her up and ask her out openly in front of everyone. A lot of men like this approach because when they get turned down they can just pretend it was a game. And turned down you will be, mainly because no barmaid is likely to say 'Yes' in front of a group of dribbling men who have all asked her the same thing 10 minutes earlier.

The brazen opener, with the quiet approach follow-up

If you really must break the ice with the brazen approach you'll have to follow up with a more sensible approach afterwards. The rules of the quiet approach kick in here, especially the cleavage one. This will require going into the pub at a quiet time without the cover of your mates. Go on, you can do it.

Should you actually get a date it's important that you realize straight away that everything that happens between you will be common knowledge. Listen, you play with fire, you get burned. You chatted her up, now deliver or face the consequences. Therefore:

☞ Take her somewhere nice enough to impress her but not somewhere your mates will laugh at later. This is like a juggling act. She'll love the theatre, but you'll never hear the end of it from your mates. Your mates will be impressed if you take her to watch boxing, but she'll never speak to you again. Just settle for another (slightly smarter) pub – you can't go wrong.

☞ Should you end up in bed, for goodness sake perform well.

The rules for women

In the interests of balance I should also list the rules for when a woman wants to ask out a barman she likes the look of:

☞ Just ask him.

'WASH YOOUR NEEM?'

Drunks and drunkenness

Pub drunks

Drunks can either be the most obnoxious characters in a pub or the most amusing. And, as is the wont of alcohol, they often morph from one to the other at a moment's notice. Some people simply steer clear of drunks, and if you are a shy, retiring type, then that is not a bad tactic. However, you will be missing out on one of the greatest joys of the pub if you do not occasionally chat to a drunk. There are endless hours of fun to be had before he (usually a he, but not always) passes out.

Trying to work out what he is saying

'Wash yoour neem?' he will repeat five times before that great moment when a drunk tries to straighten himself up as if he can shake the alcohol out of himself. This is where he stands up straight, shakes his cheeks as if to wake himself and then repeats his question really slowly. At this point, resist saying, 'Listen mate, I understood, you're just too drunk to hear my response.'

Trying to get the drunk to talk about more than one thing

Alcohol seems to fixate the mind on one topic, so if the opening conversation is about what a violation of human rights the television licence is, the rest of the conversation will be about television licences. It is great fun seeing how long you can steer the conversation in another direction before the television licence pops back up again.

Taking the piss

Drunks, of course, rarely have a clue what is going on so are open game for taking the piss. There are a few ways of doing this:

☛ Ask the drunk a stupid question, such as 'Have you ever tasted swan?' but keep a straight face. He will, remarkably, answer and you will discover it tastes a bit like chicken.

☛ Ask a really long-winded question that has no purpose, such as, 'I was on the bus the other day, do you know the people on there are so rude. My ticket cost a fortune and the seats

'Ask the drunk a stupid question, such as 'Have you ever tasted swan?' but keep a straight face. He will, remarkably, answer and you will discover it tastes a bit like chicken.'

were dirty. Do you prefer the red buses or the green ones?'
Again he will attempt an answer, although it will probably
get back to television licences before too long.

☞ Tell him a joke that has no punchline, laugh at it yourself,
then stand back and watch as he grapples with it. No one
likes to admit they don't 'get' a joke.

Be warned though, do not engage this tactic if the drunk is bigger
than you because they have a nasty habit of snapping out of
drunkenness long enough to know that the piss is being taken. If
you insist on following this route then please refer to the section
on fighting on the opposite page.

Spilling drinks

If, when you're drunk (or when you're not, for that matter) you
spill someone else's drink you should:

☞ Say sorry. You have no idea how many friends he has outside
smoking.

☞ Buy a full replacement, regardless of how much was left
or spilt. Don't try to scoop up his drink from the table or the
floor or wring it out of his top for him.

☞ Ask the bar staff for a cloth/mop/bucket so you can clean it
up. (Yes, I know that's what they are paid to do, but it doesn't
work like that. Just ask for a cloth/mop/bucket.)

Fighting in pubs

Fighting in pubs rarely actually involves punches. I know that seems a contradiction, so maybe I should rephrase: conflicts in pubs rarely actually involve punches. Whatever the *Daily Mail* says, and however scary those useless blurry CCTV images of a 'Brawl in Rochdale' are to Middle England, the reality is millions of people gather in pubs up and down the country every day and they don't all walk out with black eyes and bloody ears. Statistically, you've got a higher chance of being run over on the M62 than being bashed over the head in the Dog and Duck. (Well, I made that up, but if statistics for such things existed, I'm sure I'd be right.)

Pre-punch conflicts play themselves out in a number of ways, but essentially relate to strutting peacocks butting their chests against each other (peacocks have no arms to punch with, obviously).

Stage One

Stage One is verbal jousting, such as the gem: 'What you looking at?' While this can escalate to handbags if the other person 'bites' (i.e. reacts or acts aggressively), it's usually just a big peacock enjoying his size and is often quickly diffused with 'I'm only joking!' Everyone around breathes a sigh of relief and takes another sip of beer.

Stage Two

If the victim does bite then Stage Two kicks in. A common response to 'What are you looking at?', if you fancy a fight, would be 'Not sure, I'm still trying to work it out.' If you definitely want a fight, then insult his mother, because the golden rule of all pub verbals is that a mother's honour must be upheld, regardless of whether you've spoken to her in 20 years or not. I blame those Mafia films. Otherwise, the 'only joking' can still be applied at this stage. Everyone breathes a deep sigh of relief and takes another sip of beer.

'The golden rule of all pub verbals is that a mother's honour must be upheld, regardless of whether you've spoken to her in 20 years or not.'

Stage Three

This includes poking and pushing, along with random verbal threats about sticking various objects up various holes. The only get-out now is to pause, burst out laughing and hug the other person as if the whole thing was a joke. Use this tactic if he is considerably bigger than you, has numerous tattoos, more friends than you, or a scar on his face. Everyone breathes a huge sigh of relief, laughs nervously and takes several gulps of beer.

Stage Four

Finally … this stage includes a punch. It's rarely a clean punch, usually more of a cuff, before everyone piles in and pulls the two men apart. This is the final get-out, allowing both parties to trade insults and say 'Let me at 'im', while at the same time having no intention of actually wriggling free of their friends. After a suitable cooling-off period (about a minute) it is customary for the fighters to buy each other a pint and laugh the whole thing off. Just think of it as a convoluted way of making a new friend. Everyone else calls a halt on their heart attacks, mutters something about 'boys being boys', downs their pint and orders a whisky chaser.

'TIME, GENTLEMEN, PLEASE'

Last orders and home time

A kebab. A greasy, beautiful kebab. This is the food of the gods for drinkers after 10pm. However, now that some pubs don't shut at 11pm, the poor diehard drinkers have to wait a bit longer for their fill, but trust me, at 10pm the kebab shop starts calling.

The end of the night in a pub is a strange affair. For hours this place has been a social hub: at times a coffee shop (I still don't think that's right, though), a restaurant serving lunch and dinner, a place to meet friends and chat about the day's troubles and more. Then, come 10pm, as the beer kicks in, so does the panic. Never mind the fact pubs are open later these days, we are programmed to believe 'Closing Is At Eleven'. (Note to politicians: it'll take a generation to change mindsets so hang in there, you'll soon have the continental-style approach to alcohol of which you dream. Maybe.)

So, around 10pm the ordering gets more frenzied; strange drinks (coloured liquids and strong stuff that really should be left to the Mexicans) get added to rounds and, worst of all, the polite 'queue that no one can see but everyone knows exists' (*see* page 20) starts to disintegrate. And when the polite 'queue that no one can see but everyone knows exists' starts to disintegrate we know the nation starts to disintegrate – or so some journalists would have us believe. In my opinion, the last charge in the pub is a great tradition and can be very funny. Everyone starts talking to each other (loudly), for one thing. Granted, you might have to put up with the same conversation a few times (from the same person), but embrace this enthusiasm for talking to strangers because it's one of the few times it's allowed in this country. More often than not, the closing of a pub on a busy weekend night follows a regular pattern:

Stage One

Everyone is drinking and enjoying themselves quietly:

☞ Groups of people are keeping themselves to themselves

☞ Boys' shirts have that creased, thanks-for-the-iron look

☞ Girls' skirts reach down to their thighs

Stage Two

The start of chaos. What sparks this is a variety of factors. Drinking time is running out, alcohol is kicking in, the music is starting to get into everyone's bones. The pub bewitching hour is upon us.

☞ The first mention of 'kebab/curry' is heard

☞ The first mention of 'club' is heard

☞ The first protestation of 'I have to work in the morning' is used

☞ The first tequilas are ordered

☞ One of the group talks to someone from another group – that's it, the floodgates have opened.

Stage Three

The embrace of chaos. Time is ticking.

☞ More tequilas are ordered (one for the curvy girl you've been too shy to talk to for the last three hours)

☞ The debate over kebab or curry is intensifying

☞ The girl who has to work in the morning is losing the argument

☞ The beautifully ironed shirts start to get drinks spilled on them

☞ Groups who have been eyeing each other start to mingle and love is in the air

☞ A few silly words are spoken – 'Just leave it' is heard more than once

☞ The guv'nor starts looking at the clock.

Stage Four

Chaos has taken hold. The moment all guv'nors, sober people and foreigners dread. Britain at its best.

☞ There are more tequilas than answers

☞ The polite 'queue that no one can see but everyone knows exists' has disappeared. This is no time for politeness.

☞ The group has decided that it's a kebab followed by a club but a couple of them are going for a curry, 'whatever anyone else wants to do'.

☞ Snogging has begun

☞ Married couples are remembering the days

☞ The odd bit of pushing and shoving is brewing

☞ Hugging is allowed by all and sundry

☞ Taxi drivers start to appear

☞ 'Last orders ladies and gentlemen' is heard ringing around the pub. Some advanced-thinking places may even send a staff member around to warn people who have become deaf through tequila and singing that the bell has been rung.

☞ Loud and very bad singing while hanging onto the shoulders of your friends (and newly made friends) is now permitted, as is holding a make-believe microphone to your lips – although air guitar is still a step too far.

Stage Five

Chaos takes over the pub. Would you like another tequila?

☞ Hugging spreads. Hug your friends, hug that girl/guy you've always fancied, hug a stranger, just bloody hug someone.

Straight men must still retain a stiff upper body and pat each other firmly on the back to prove their hetero-ness, while women can do what they want in the hugging stakes. Men start queuing up hoping their luck is in.

☞ One or two people are really hungry now

☞ Drinks pile up on the tables and no one knows who owns what

☞ Regardless of the above, people keep on ordering, despite cries of 'I don't want another one!'

- You will spot a hand up a skirt

- The last taxi man is getting increasingly irate as he can't find his fare

- Groups start chatting to the bouncers in bigger pubs (the previously invisible bald blobs in badly cut black suits)

- The clever ones in the group argue over the meaning of 'alliteration' on the quiz machine

- 'Time, ladies and gentlemen!' is heard (by some)

- Bar staff prepare for the long goodbye.

Stage Six

Goodbye to chaos. Hello to complete chaos.

- The lights go on. They are really bright and everyone has to squint

- The music is turned down

- Everyone asks, 'Can I get another drink?'

- 'Go on,' they insist. 'Just one.'

- The clever ones shoot off early to get in the queue for the kebab/curry. There are not many of them.

☞ Everyone else keeps asking for a late beer/tequila/vodka

☞ Romantic pairings are being finalized (although if someone nips to the toilet there is still a chance for a late change)

☞ Goodbye huggings commence

☞ The odd fight might break out. 'Silly boys,' everyone says, except a couple of girls turned on by such bravado.

☞ Bar staff walk around reminding everyone with three pints, two tequilas and a vodka and Coke that they have three minutes to drink up.

☞ The bar staff come back a minute later

☞ And again

☞ A skinny boy in a Ted Baker T-shirt downs a third of a pint, slams down his glass and exclaims, 'There, you happy?!'

☞ The bar staff get abused

☞ Everyone leaves, including the last taxi man, who will now take anyone who will pay

☞ The bar staff say 'Good fucking riddance.' Probably.

Stage Seven

And so to bed all pub-goers young and old.

☞ Sometimes with a sexy stranger

☞ Usually with a bit of kebab hanging just below the left side of your bottom lip.

Don't you just love British pubs?